# Blessed With a Broken Heart

*Blessed With a Broken Heart* is a journey through personal experiences with moments of lows and highs.

An internal monologue took the form of poems because, in order to cope with everything, words began to form in isolation. After the discovery at a very young age that the idea of imperfection is embedded in the human soul and mind, the idealised image of parents and loved ones started changing and things took on a different hue.

*Blessed With a Broken Heart* is a steep upward journey that started when health and life hit rock bottom. It is the story of how one can carry oneself out of a dark space, hold people accountable, move on from detrimental experiences and onto a steadier plateau. It is a brave attempt at showcasing experiences, memories, strength and an internal war against the past.

# BLESSED WITH A BROKEN HEART

SANAYA Y IRANI

An imprint of Manjul Publishing House Pvt. Ltd.
• C-16, Sector 3, Noida, Uttar Pradesh 201 301, India
Website: www.manjulindia.com

*Registered Office:*
• 2nd Floor, Usha Preet Complex, 42 Malviya Nagar,
Bhopal 462 003 – India

*Distribution Centres*
Ahmedabad, Bengaluru, Chennai, Hyderabad,
Kochi, Kolkata, Mumbai, Noida, Pune

*Blessed With a Broken Heart* by Sanaya Y Irani



This edition published in paperback by
Amaryllis, an imprint of Manjul Publishing House in 2025

**ISBN 978-93-5543-782-2**

Cover & inside illustrations: Sanaya Y Irani

Printed and bound in India by Repro India Limited

To the ones we love, the ones we lost
and the ones we loathe

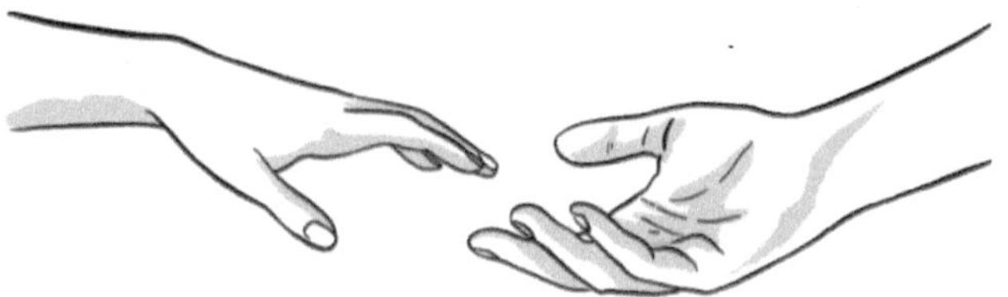

# Contents

*Allowing*

Bad Things 3
Cradling Chaos 4
Saviour 6
Love 7
Purpose 9
Rooms 10
Provider 12
Walls 13
Staircase 14
Criticism 16
Hours of the Night 17
Stories 18
Narcissism 19
Open Book 21
Tears of Silk 22
Grief 23
Letting Go 25
The Terrible Tragedy of My Thoughts 26
Imagination 28
Hell in Hello 29
Rain Showers 30

*Realising*

Seven Kingdoms 33
On My Mind 34

Price of Peace 36
Blood on My Hands 37
Déjà Vu 38
At the Gate 40
Noise 41
Footprints 42
Neglect 43
Contempt 44
Boats 45
Too Much 46
Man Enough 48
Felt 50
How Are You? 51
Hollow 53
Mere Thieves 54
The Sunday 55
Harm Me 58
New Low 59
Unsure 60

*Understanding*

Mirrors 65
Loneliness 67
Inconsistencies 69
Lilies 70
Excuses 71
Father's Daughter 72
Honesty 74
Come and Go 75
Silence 77
Nothing 78

Duties of a Daughter 80
Sweet Poison 82
Shade of Rain 83
Losses 85
Wake Up Happy 86
Remedies for the Spirit 87
Apologies 88
Who I Am 89
Ignorance is Bliss 91
No One's Watching 92
Atrocities 93

*Accepting*

Normal 97
Cliché 99
Examples 100
Actions 102
To Be Heard 103
Chances 105
101 Ways to Die 106
You're Next 108
Woman 109
Someone Like You 110
Deathbed 111
BPD 112
Little of You 113
I Cry, I Cry 114
Vase 116
Growth 117
Women 119
Ties 120

Afraid to Fall 121
Parts of Me 122
Mother 124

## *Adapting*

Slow journey 129
Listen 130
The Little Things 132
I Remember 134
I Think of You 137
Patience 139
Hold On 140
Intimacy 141
Moments 142
Directions 144
You 145
To Be an Artist 146
Sisters 148
Meant for Me 150
Breaks You 151
What I Want 152
Physical Touch 153
Balloons 155
I Am Home 156
Compliment Her Strength 158
Friendships 159
Finger on the Trigger 160
Strangers 161
What Leaves 162
Closure 163
Undo It All 166

I’s In Love 167
The Mother in Me 168

*About the Author* 171

# *Allowing*

When I was a child I knew bad things can ruin good people
Now, I also know bad people can ruin good things.

# Cradling Chaos

Chaos is the cradle I was raised in,
Noise is the only silence I had,
Broken were all bonds after witnessing sin,
Ignorance is bliss and that's why I'm sad.

I know too much and I forgot to forget,
I walk around bearing resentment,
I wake up unwillingly afraid and yet,
I strive for daily contentment.

Chaos is gentle music to my ears,
I fade into background noise,
Disassociation is a superpower,
Violence is closer than grace and poise.

My triggers exist all around me,
I wait anxious till you step on the mine,
I was taught to control my reactions and see,
How well I can pretend like I'm fine.

I breathe and slip away into the dark night,
For I have dreams and funerals to attend,
Chaos is the cradle I was raised in and,
That's where I'll lie in the end.

## *Saviour*

There you go again,
solving problems that you didn't create
Closing doors you didn't open
Feeding mouths you didn't birth
Protecting secrets that aren't yours
And building houses you can't live in
Are you the saviour?
Or are you hoping someone will notice you're in need of saving?

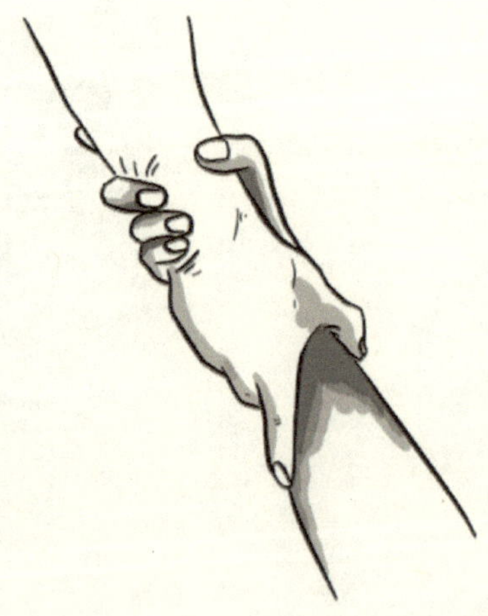

What is love?
Love doesn't have a definition,
It isn't an object ready for proclamation.
Love is the cyclone that waited to destroy every thought in my mind
that I claimed to be sane.
Love is the mixture of the simplicity in my footsteps
towards that person and the complexity of the rush I feel
within my stomach crushing itself with ecstasy.
Love is incomprehensible and simultaneously the easiest thing to understand for the person drowning in it.
Love is the wave crushing me down while I take care of the glistening pearl resting on the sea bed.
Love is everything I wish for and wish everything for.
Yet love is the sweetest poison that I'll ever taste and the coldest warmth I'll ever feel.

Love is not just a feeling.
Love is the rarest emotion to find and the easiest to lose.
I'm not in it and it isn't around me,
I am so lost in the concept of love, lost enough to be unable to decipher reality and imagination.
Love for me isn't a four letter word,
It is a journey from the moment I tripped on those fluttering lashes
of the mesmerizing eyes that gazed upon me to the countless infinities
I make up that lie before me.
Then again,
How could I know what love is?
For I can't see a thing,
And they say love is blind.

When will you learn that saving your mum and being good enough for your dad isn't your sole purpose in this life?

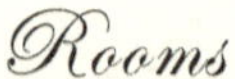

I've tried reasoning with others.
I've tried for moments upon moments to take up spaces in rooms
that were made two sizes too small for me.
by people who smirked and shamed me for being different and detached.

I've held onto hope, wishing I wasn't the only one who wore the garland of embarrassment every time I was myself in front of them.
I've heard to err is human but if only they didn't distil the truth
and leave out how loud the sound of your mistakes are when everyone is waiting in silence for you to make them.

Waiting to spend another hurtful sentence at your expense.
I have sat in chairs of lies pulled out for me not knowing
they are made from the soft feathers of deceit
and ill intent, wrapped up in satin sheets of sarcasm,
at the very table where your personality is picked on
and pulled up for everyone to take aim and fire.

I've let those I held in high regard look down upon
me as I lay down the carpet only for them to walk all over me.

I have questioned my existence and emotions
because I felt like I was the only body in the room being scanned.

Rehearsing my steps before I took them, repeating my sentences before I said them.

How many mistakes can you allow yourself to make
when you think you are one to begin with?

I tried reasoning with others,
In spaces that weren't mine
Till I ran out of reasons
And they ran out of time.

## *Provider*

you were a provider yes, but you didn't provide an ounce of love.
You were a protector yes, but you harmed me the most.
You were the sole earner yes, but you didn't earn my respect.
You were a defender yes, but where were you when I was being preyed upon?

You were everything to me,
Till you made sure you were nothing.

You were supposed to be the saviour,
And I was in need of saving.

But I had to save myself.

I have walked through life with the walls caving in on me
You couldn't possibly burden me.

## *Staircase*

I'm too dark to lighten up.
There's an endless flight of stairs to get to how low I feel,
A tunnel under the basement of my feelings leads up to the empty carcass of what I once was,
barely breathing, laying among the nightmares that consumed me;

I don't let people visit this place,
for they wouldn't believe how much darkness there is behind this curtain of rainbows
and how weak my knees are from standing up to myself.

They say I have so much to be happy for,
If only I knew how to stay happy
In my head
It's back and forth like a relay of emotions
I stumble and scrape myself
There is no first aid in sight, maybe I love to hurt myself

They say be brave you have so much to live for,
If only I knew what that meant
In my heart.

I'm stone cold in a straightjacket
But I don't seem to be struggling,
There is no end in sight,

I'd rather be tied up than let my mind run free.

Why does criticism come to you easier than compassion?

# *Hours of the Night*

My pillows have heard confessions
And my blanket has known sorrow,
While I wept and screamed silently
Into the unseen morrow,
And when I woke, I left my bed
For the sun, she shines so bright,
Drying up the tears shed
During the hours of the night.

Stories spoken with vengeful deceit shall always unveil themselves to be false when the person speaking them turns out to be guilty.

*Let time handle it.*

# Narcissism

The devil comes in all sizes,
None too big and none too small,
For malice breeds in narcissism,
Where there lies no love at all.

Foresight left in ruins,
No one can warn you about the lies,
You can never be too careful,
Not too ignorant nor too wise.

Self-esteem buried,
Lips sealed all too tight,
Hands tied behind you,
And no will left to fight.

Held on as prisoner,
Because the bad was followed by good,
All in a day's haze,
And leave you never could.

You watch silently on,
As years pass you by,
Till you walked away one day,
With that freeing goodbye.

Life moves on slowly,
Barely anyone left to call,
No way to define love,
When you've seen no love at all.

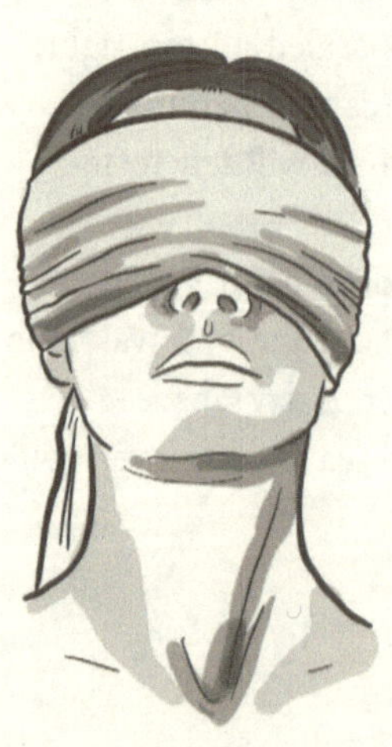

I was the open book you chose to scribble in.

The tears of silk that run down your face
could make up nine yards of a saree full of lies.

# Grief

I have waited to grieve.
To be a person who lay so far below the ground
That my screams would be buried like the memories of my past.
I waited so long to grieve the death of my inner child,
it's been months since I last pretended
to be the mask of a happy person.

I grieve the loss of the moments I can't remember,
I grieve the presence of the moments I want to forget.
I have learnt of heavy secrets
And I have forgotten little joys
I grieve the loss of the weakness that I held onto,
I grieve gaining the strength to push through the pain.

I am consumed by grief for that is all I have known for a while.
I have choked on gratitude
Saying 'it could get worse' while it progressively did.
I have seen death, I have walked to and
Lived in the moments before it.

I have seen death steal the light from a loved one's eyes.
I have felt warm blood go cold and soft hands go stiff.
I have felt grief fill in every vein of my body till my heart bled for them.

I have sat in cars of anxiety. Walked on pavements of guilt.
I have taken elevators down to depression.
I have entered rooms of fear and visited pain too often.
I have learnt to live with grief and embrace it.

Like an old friend. Like an old enemy.

Thank you for letting go because
I would've gifted you the noose to hang me with.

# *The Terrible Tragedy of My Thoughts*

I have been shown love through violence,
I, as a woman have been praised for my silence,
I have been told we should be seen and not heard,
I have been told men had the final word.

I have been told to make use of myself,
I have been touched and silenced at twelve,
I was told that family protects you,
but fam, I need protection from you.

I have wounds I don't speak out for,
I have contemplated ending it before,
I have been told my depression was fake,
By the same person who got depressed when we took a break.

I have had cuts on my heart and hands,
I have stood where no daughter should stand,
I have had to choose silence for their success,
In turn making my own heart a giant mess.

I have seen the world rotate for too long,
I feel like my soul is just dragging along,
I haven't felt awakened and I don't feel alive
Because so many shattered my inner child.

I was too loud, too crazy and too stubborn for one,
I was too melancholy and too low for some,
I spoke too much and put my heart on the table,
Only to constantly get fucking labelled.

So where must I put my angry bitter spirit?
Her head and her heart need rest for a minute.
And while she rests I'll tell you how she fought,
Welcome to the terrible tragedy of my thoughts.

My imagination is so good,
I mistook you for a blessing.

Baby with you, there's hell in every hello.

I love rain showers,
For when I stand in them,
My tears look just like rain.

# Realising

How dare you promise us seven kingdoms
when you sold our own home to begin with.

## *On My Mind*

There's so many different things I could say when they ask me what's on my mind,
A million billion open tabs yet an answer seems hard to find.

Should I describe the nightmare I had where I fell off a height?
Should I talk about my fear of love & my attachment to the silent night?

Must I open up about my trauma or make small talk just for fun?
Have I told them about what I do for a living
and how much I hate to run?

Did I mention I hate awkward silence when two people are in an empty space?
Am I too loud when I fill that in, with words I can't erase?

Should I mention how intrigued I am to know what lies beneath the deep blue water?
Is it too much to cry and bring up how much I hated being a daughter?

Do they need to know about my life and the decisions that I made?
Do they know if death comes knocking, I won't be afraid?

Very little comes to my tongue when my brain floods with thoughts,
I wish sometimes I could stay silent & they would connect the dots.

I talk a lot for someone who barely says what I'm thinking,
I dream of swimming in open conversations but really, I'm only sinking.

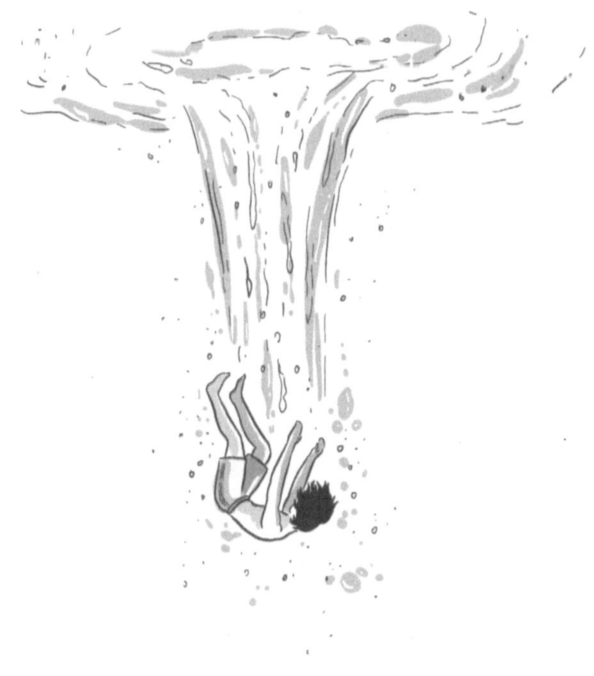

# Price of Peace

I have allowed myself to feel, to fall, to stand, to break
I have let myself breathe,
I have paid in memories, dreams and tears to get to where I stand.
I smiled in difficult times to show courage,
I choked on my pride for peace.
I held back my opinions when they cringed,
I cried in silent rooms and car rides for peace.

The peace I bought, left me in debt.
It left me laying under weighted blankets of my own repressed feelings.
It made my knees buckle to the floor, and now they're bruised for peace.
I kept my thoughts to myself,
I burnt pages of what I wrote hoping my feelings would go up in flames.
I tore books hoping my words wouldn't follow me,
I shattered mirrors hoping my reflection wouldn't hurt me.

I stayed silent for peace, I screeched into my pillow for peace.
If only they knew the price of peace.
Everything I did for peace.

*Oh how I wish, I could finally rest in peace.*

You say I have blood on my hands;
All I asked you for was the truth,
And you slit my wrists instead.

And you say I have blood on my hands.

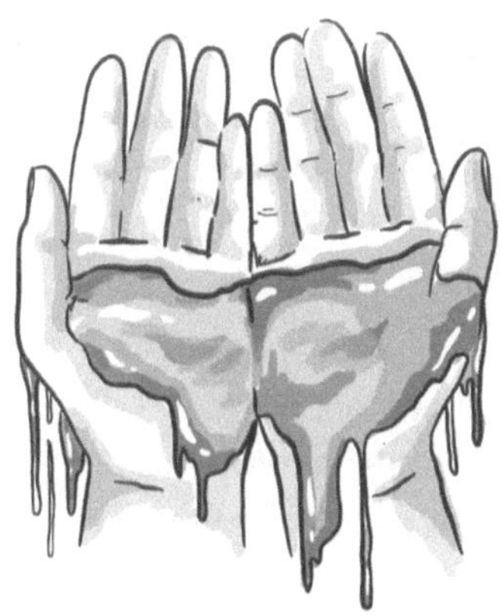

# Déjà Vu

I am in a room of broken mirrors,
Torn paintings on the floor,
Crushed dreams lying across the hall,
I've been here before.

I looked into the wardrobe,
The clothes, the smallest in every store,
Health dangling on the hangers,
I've been here before.

I sit at the table silently,
Hazy memories with my family of four,
Too scared to say the next wrong thing,
I've been here before.

I walk past the room with loud noises,
All I hear is disagreements through the door,
They call for help, it's not my place,
I've been here before.

What appears next is a school,
Skinned me alive to the very core,
Not an ounce of self-esteem to carry into the world,
I've been here before.

I walk past people I used to trust,
No signs of belief anymore,
My spine tired of standing up for
myself,
I've been here before.

I lay down contemplating my choices,
Most of which I deplore,
I am my biggest enemy,
I've been here before.

I push my heels into the ground,
And stand up once more,
With all and everything I have in me,
I've been here before.

My mind paints the world colourful,
And I have so much of it to explore,
Moments and memories I need to arrive to,
Places I have never been before.

# *At the Gate*

She woke up and out of bed tired from last night's dream
She panicked her way through the roads of rage she paved
She crawled beneath the heavy boulders of her anxiety
To reach the gates of judgement she built.
He awaited her on the other side where the grass felt greener,
Where people weren't meaner,
She thought he'd seen her.

She walked closer to see,
The boy was a shadow of her imagination, a mere mirage,
There stood a mirror:
Looking back at her she saw a face of bitterness, someone she once loved but now loathed, someone she once recognised but now, behold:
She didn't have to find love in a man,
She had to look deep inside herself

*And that was further than anyone had ever dared to go.*

Why do I crave silence when I am the noise?

## *Footprints*

I'm writing a poem for you. You the carefree traveller,
You who walked into my cage of cushions, uncalled for and unknown

I was mouldable and frail, an offer you ought to avail.
I took you as you led me to believe and I couldn't be more naive.

You walked right to me, you walked right through me you left your trail.

A trail that led me to the edge of insanity.
Your curtain of love existed only to cover up your inhumanity.

Your footstep was unique, it felt soulful and deep.
It felt like a size ten on the feel scale, the real fucking deal scale.

And now I arrive at my dead end, it's my time to fight or fly
I'm adapting to each day as it fleetingly passes me by

I lay here today as I have a footprint etched deep in me
I walk the path of solitude watching the endless skies and sea

I believe there are miracles and they will come in due time
I will find a footprint to finally walk side by side with mine.

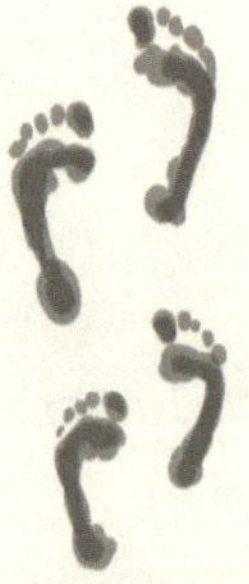

# *Neglect*

One day you bring a flowering plant home:
find out all about its needs,
show it off to your friends,
shower it with water daily,
call it your best plant yet,
and then water it lesser everyday,
till you don't water it at all,
and it starts to wilt and die.

I always wondered why you had
so many empty pots and dying plants when you got me home
but only the cactus survived.

She calls it love. I call it neglect.

I'd hold you in contempt of courting me
I'd be the jury, the victim and the judge.

I gaze upon the boats
On the shore of our island,
One stuck so deep in the sand
While the other floats,
Because I kept coming back here
Not knowing if you'd return,
But I have my answer I fear.

## *Too Much*

I've heard of the saying:

'If I'm too much, go find less'
And gosh, I do agree,
But I don't think less will suit you anymore
Because you got too much from me.

You'll wander shore to shore
Looking for the boat you missed,
Water won't quench your thirst anymore
For you tasted love when we kissed.

You looked me deep in the eye
Whispered sweet nothings to me,
I held you close, watched you cry,
But that's not how you like it to be.

Shallow graves keep you warm,
You won't let anyone dig that deep
Maybe what they find, you fear,
Isn't what they'd like to keep.

Vulnerability makes you a fast runner
Maybe it's your competitive side,
I wish I could remind you, however,
You can't outrun what lies inside.

The oceans we built in the time we had
Are now barren and bone dry,
I'd fill them back up again, you see,
But I promised I wouldn't cry.

I have seen what love could look like
And what love should never be,
And I know nothing you ask in love
Would ever be too much for me.

But foolish fools get fooled
Destiny declares it such
I hope we never meet again
And I hope that's not too much.

## *Man Enough*

I was man enough to be strong,
hold my own weight,
open my own doors,
buy my own flowers
and drop myself places.

I was man enough to speak my truth,
state my needs,
make the first move
and pay for some meals

I was man enough to make plans
to show interest
to solve conflict
and to communicate clearly.

But,

I should've been feminine enough to say no,
to walk away,
to stop at the first red flag,
to not let you disrespect me.

I should've been feminine enough
to put myself first sometimes,
to allow myself to have a life outside of you,
to be less available to you,

I should've been feminine enough to feel safe around you,
to trust you around others,
to be myself around you,
to not break down in sheer panic with you.

I would've been feminine if
I wasn't too busy
being more of a man than you ever were.

I wish you felt how I did
and didn't just touch me.

## *How Are You?*

When someone asks me how I'm doing,
I take a breath and say,
As good as I can and will be
Better than I was yesterday.

For who has the bandwidth to explain
What my feelings are all about,
'You have it much better than others'
The tone-deaf wait to shout.

They question my basic sanity
When I say I want to die,
No one cares to look for reasons
When, what happened and why?

My childhood took from me
More than thieves can and ever will,
Trust, innocence & self-worth
And a reason to be alive still.

I gave up a long time ago
Putting myself first and all,
It's a pattern that's hard to let go of
When you're always pushed to take the fall.

Words don't comfort me
And hugs never could,
I've found trust is hard to come by
And feelings are always misunderstood.

There's a way to be honest still
And save all of your time,
People seldom ask you questions
Once you've told them you're fine.

How can someone be full of themselves
and still so hollow?

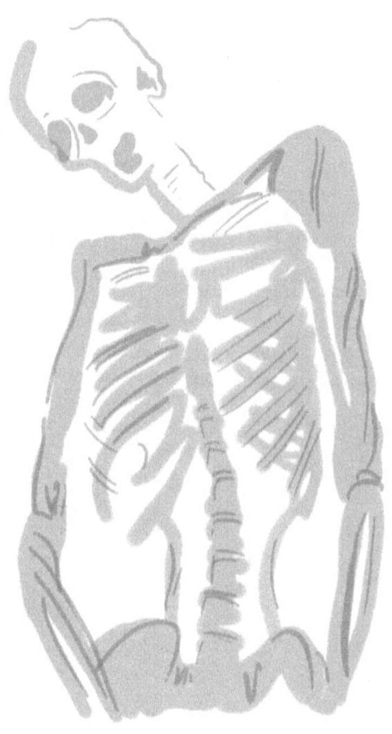

I opened my heart out to people
And
Let them borrow what they please
None of it returned or reciprocated,
All of them, mere thieves.

## *The Sunday*

I am all the people I have met,
I am all the conversations I've had,
I am the one who stays too long,
and I'm the best he says he's had.

I am the one who holds your hand,
The one who drops herself home,
The one who pretends like she's not bothered,
By the girls you meet alone.

I am the one to hear you vent,
I am always one call away,
I am the symphony of reasoning,
And for your success, I pray.

I am the one who gave you chances,
to prove your actions matched your words,
I felt the blood trickle down my spine,
when I heard what I heard.

So now let me tell you,

I am not one to stand by,
While you lie, bury and hide,
I shall not put my blind love for you,
Above my own dignity and pride.

You've put down your friends
behind their backs,
At every chance you've got,
You complain about your family,
Like you're the smartest and they're not.

Your past can't seem to stay behind you,
You're the one that 'always comes back',
Must be nice for your lovers turned sisters,
To validate the feelings you lack.

You read books on persuasion,
You study how to be a friend,
You try tricks and manipulations,
So that they may like you enough to bend.

You have your way with words,
You may look charismatic when you bloom,
But there will always be one,
Who can sense your mask in that room.

I knew who you were, all too familiar,
When I started to fall,
You reminded me of home,
Where there was no love at all.

I begged you till it burned me,
From the inside out,
How many times can I whisper,
When you don't even hear me shout?

You failed to do right by me,
And I couldn't digest you well,
My chest, my stomach, my nerves,
All fought till it felt like hell.

So I picked up my heart from you,
The day you said you were done,
We always fought for who loved the other more,
And that Sunday, I won.

If you were a flower, you'd be a rose
If an insect, you'd be a bee
You look pretty from a distance, yes
But if I come close,

*You'd do more harm than good to me.*

## *New Low*

I look at you in wonder
And take mental pictures of your smile,
I can't imagine you do the same
Maybe it's not worth your while.

I have spoken about you constantly
To friends and family who are now sick.
You're on my mind incessantly
And I'd love you through thin and thick.

I've pushed myself off cliffs for you
And I've hit a brand new low,
I can't stop, nor do I want to
If it was easy then I'd just let go.

One sided love agrees with a few
And I'm diving deeper into that pit,
Plenty offer words of advice
But I still choose to swim in *shit.*

## *Unsure*

If you are unsure, ask yourself:
How do they make me feel?

Are they soft, gentle and kind?
Do they expect you to read their mind?
Can they talk and communicate?
Do they always seem to make you wait?
Do they show you love and care?
Are they apathetic and unaware?
Can they respect you and your friends?
Do they drop you home when the night ends?
Are they consistent and worth your trust?
Do you feel like an object of lust?
Can they be honest and true about their past?
Are they still attached to the person they dated last?
Can your body rest with them in the room?
Does your gut feel a sense of impending doom?
Are they working on themselves and their past trauma?
Do they call your emotions overacting or drama?
Do they reassure you when you may be low?
Do they give you mixed signals while they come and go?
Do they make your stomach tingle and your head dizzy?
Do they always make excuses and say they're too busy?
Can they turn up for you at the drop of a hat?
Do they gaslight you with 'I never said that'?
Are they the same person you knew 3 months back?
Have they ever caused a panic attack?

Do they encourage you and celebrate your wins?
Do you feel like you're walking around them on eggshells and pins?
Do they ask you questions about your day?
Do their actions back the words they say?
Do you two have a lot in common?
Do you only need validation from them?
Are you allowing yourself to live and do as you please?
Do you go out with them and feel at ease?
Has there been a moment with them when you felt your heart sink?
Do they cause you to constantly overthink?
Have they ever called you names and made you feel bad?
Have they blamed their bad behaviour on past problems they had?

Do you feel like their ego prevents them from being their higher self?
Do you think they worship money and only focus on their wealth?
Can you see them returning the love you gave them?
Are you making excuses for their behaviour and protecting them?
Do you see them as they are and not as if they were better?
Do they buy you flowers and write you love letters?

Now step back for me and take a second to imagine.

If you came across this in your own child's book
Mistook this for a fun quiz and had a quick look
If you read all the questions and how you answered them
Would you be happy or terrified for them?

Would you allow your child to feel how you do?
Or would you only allow this to happen to you?

# Understanding

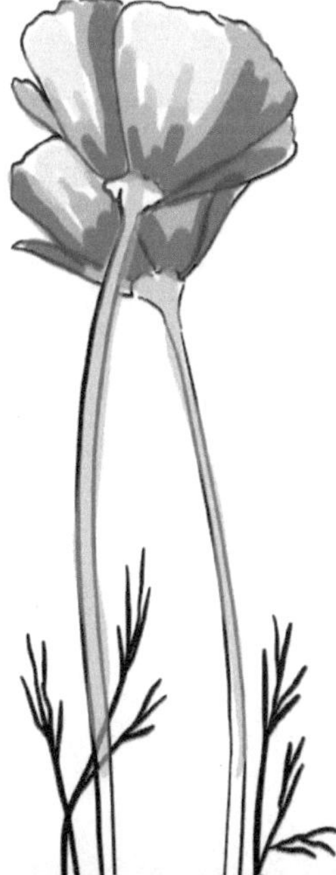

## *Mirrors*

I pushed my face up against the mirror
the absolute closest I could get,
I picked at all my insecurities,
and cried till my cheeks were wet.

I cringed, I cursed, I complained,
I fed myself the worst words there were,
I looked at every other person,
and wished I was a little more like her.

When I grew up, I broke out, turned red,
My body walked a line so thin,
My appetite lessened and I was okay,
since I was complimented for being so slim.

They wanted my body while my skin clung onto my bones,
I could see my ribs in my reflection,
I got tattoos and piercings to express myself,
and so my eyes could have a distraction.

I hated the way I looked,
and comments from people just broke me down,
I took the rage, the frustration and pain,
I swallowed it all without a sound.

My mirror was my worst enemy,
I had to gather all my pieces after the fall,
I look at myself now with empathy,
for I am healing and growing to love my all.

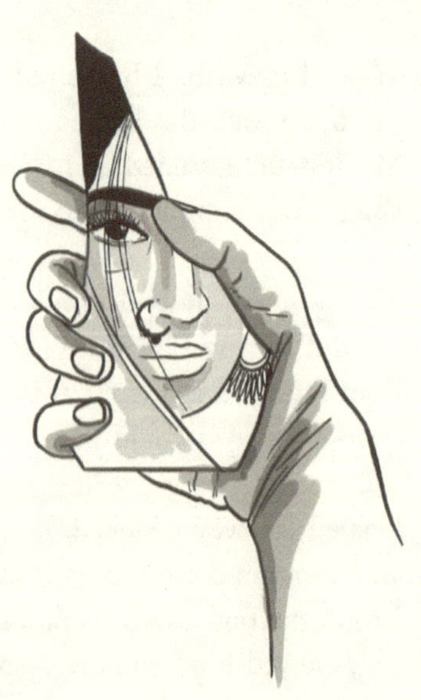

## *Loneliness*

When I first started off in life
I had plenty of friends,
One for every day of the week,
And triple for the weekends.

Moving up a few grades
And after changing some seats around,
Most of them grouped away,
And some left town.

I had a new best friend in every class
None permanent whatsoever,
I peaked in high school and dipped right after,
Many left after saying 'forever'.

I made new promises in college
Only a handful this time around,
Some etched their name in my heart,
And some faded in the background.

Today I look back and wonder
Most of everyone I knew was a lesson,
There was much to learn back then
Only if I had paid attention.

I have myself today and less than 5 that truly know me,
Most of the time I'm alone but I'm never truly lonely.

Inconsistencies are the root cause of disbelief.

## *Lilies*

When I walked past the lilies today,
I held onto them for dear life,
I didn't know if I was dreaming or here to stay,
I didn't know if I was dead or alive.

Lilies reminded me of you,
The way they bloomed for me,
When the tears ran down my face,
I watered them accidentally.

I attached some part of myself to you,
like the lilies that stained everything I wore,
maybe letting you in was a mistake,
I should've left your flowers at the door.

But when I walked past the lilies today,
Some part of me broke and bled,
I knew the lilies were no longer mine,
And that part of me was dead.

If you want to, you'll find a way
If you don't, you'll find an excuse

## *Father's Daughter*

I wasn't really a father's daughter,
As much as I'd have liked to be,
We were so different but almost too similar,
I could see a lot of him in me.

We spoke in questions
And sat in different rooms,
I carried a knife to cut through the tension
And he had a hammer, I presume.

There was so much anger lingering throughout,
My mind was a volatile place,
I kept my voice low till I began to shout
And you could see the resentment on my face.

We moved from arguments to conversations,
I told him every day about how I felt,
If I think back now and make observations,
I knew somewhere his hard exterior began to melt.

It was a bond that required healing,
And heal we did somehow,
We found common interests and some things appealing,
We were repairing ourselves, if I think about it now

He didn't love through physical touch,
Rather acts of service and subtle gift giving,
He didn't believe in words of affirmation or even quality time that much,
I understand that now and I'm so forgiving.

It's too late for me now to tell him the words I think,
It's a bit too soon to give in to how I feel,
I always think of him when I'm at the brink
And now I live with the truth of what is real.

He means so much to me and now lies far away,
I see him in my reflections in the stagnant water,
You would not believe how much I think of him night and day,
I truly do miss being my father's daughter.

## *Honesty*

Even if I searched the corners of the earth
I wouldn't find a single morsel of honesty
in the promises you made to me.

What hurts isn't how you broke them,
it is the ease with which you made them,

*They were mere shallow words to you.*

# Come and Go

You come and go like the waves of the indecisive
sea,
you come and go like the intrusive thoughts on
my mind,
you've gone back and forth like a child on a
swing,
and you appear like things I lost and couldn't
find.

you were here and left like footprints in
the sand,
you were here and left like money I lost
on bad bets,
you've brought joy and taken more than you
came with,
somehow all I have left is a heavy bag of regrets.

you come and go like crosswinds through
my door,
you come and go and keep me wishing for
more,
you did everything right but you came and went
away,

you did so much in so little time
and you did everything but stay.

The silence I live in now
Is better than the silence I had while talking to you.

I am alone now,
*But not as lonely as I was with you.*

# *Nothing*

I want to be a fragment of their imagination,
I want to cease to exist,
I want to undo my creation,
I want to be a memory, just a gist.

I want nothing from this world
and not a single thought to be true,
I want no truth unfurled
and not a word of comfort from you.

I want to lay down and not rise from this plateau,
I want to feel the soil cover me whole,
I want to be nothing but a shadow,
I want back nothing that they stole.

I want the ground from under me broken
like the ribs under my skin,
I want to silence the words I have spoken
and muffle the voices within.

I want to breathe a sigh of relief,
I want to cleanse myself from need,
I want a release from the grief,
I want to walk away from greed.

I want freedom from fear,
I want to melt in the rain,
I want nothing and no one dear,
I want to make peace with my pain.

## *Duties of a Daughter*

I have the duties of a daughter
That my father left to me,
He didn't plan on dying
And passing stuff on, you see.

I picked up the shattered pieces
Of my family split in two,
There was enough damage done
More than I could ever do.

When the pillar and the provider
All fall within the night,
It's harder than you plan-
To see the tunnel and the light.

Your perceptions change
And so do your plans,
Nothing seems to be in your control;
Not one thing in your hands.

I get back up off my knees
And dust my mindset right through,
You let go of what you can't control
And you don't let it control you.

Life tends to get easier with time
And I am a testament to that fact,
You must shed the weight of the world
That you carry on your back.

So with the duties of a daughter,
I carry on living,
The universe is the teacher,
And the gift that keeps on giving.

I have forgotten what you were to me,
a sweet poison or the bitter remedy.

## *Shade of Rain*

What shade of rain would I be?

I look out the window while it rains
Each drop pouring incessantly,
I wonder in deep thought
What shade of the rain I could be.

Would I be the scarce morning sprinkle
That lands on your face so light?
The roses feel the dewdrops
And the sun would still be bright.

Would I be the brisk afternoon rain
That you could still run through?
No need for raincoats or covers
I'd just be annoying to you.

Would I be the nasty 5 min pour
That gets you drenched and wet?
You wish you hadn't gotten out
And now you're full of regret.

Or would I be the night-long steady rain
That keeps you worried throughout?
Stressed about life tomorrow
And I'd fill your plans with doubt.

Maybe I'd be the storm that stays
And never lets you leave,
You'd be shaking and deaf with the thunder
And with the lightning up my sleeve.

What if I was the rain that never came,
What if I left you high and dry?
No sign of me, no word from me,
Not a cloud in the sky.

But I'd like to be the gentle shower,
The one with the rainbow shining through,
I'd water your fields and fill your wells,
I'd pour my heart out for you.

Why do you scream out your losses
and whisper your victories?

*There is no prize for being your biggest hater.*

I am the forgotten memory
that will replay in your mind right before you wake
and you will spend the rest of the day
wondering why you woke up *happy*.

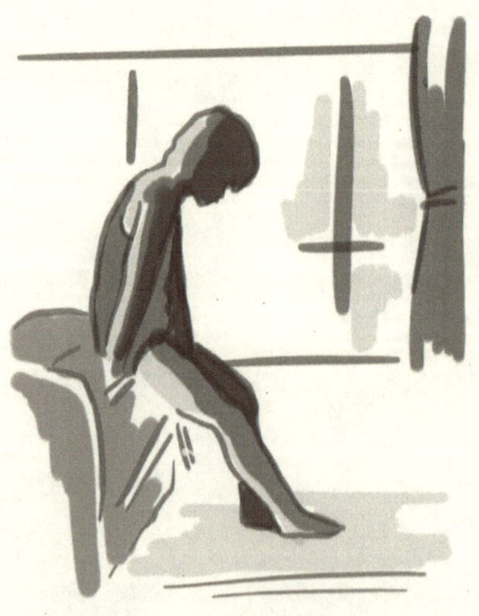

# Remedies for the Spirit

I have remedies for the spirit
they lie inside me like the shy child in 2nd grade who only spoke once a day.

I carry all my solutions or so I've been told.
I am the cure and the cause to everything I have suffered from but I don't remember signing up for this.

I have remedies for the spirit like the medicine box I only opened after being terribly sick for a while.
I have remedies but I seem to be drawn to sickness.
I am the doctors note and the medicine she wrote, I am the unreadable text.
I am all of the pills stocked in the chemist but they have surpassed their expiry date.

I have remedies for the spirit in a jar tightly shut that only my own father can open.
I have remedies for the spirit in a jar that my own father sealed shut.

The number of times you apologised to me
but I had to keep making changes
really goes to show how love never works
when it's *one-sided.*

# *Who I Am*

I make up my mother's memories,
I am my father's fears,
I am the belly full of laughter,
I am the bucket of tears.

I mould into the concepts you have,
I am the delusional thought,
I am the distance before damage,
I am the battle fought.

I breathe in the consequence,
I am the stepping stone,
I am the compass guide,
I am the way home.

I walk the path of wisdom,
I am the balancing weight,
I am the all or nothing,
I am up for debate.

I plough the seeds of sorrow,
I am the lingering spirit,
I am your desires and your dreams,
I am the land and everything in it.

I fuel the fire and the flame,
I am the dull night,
I am the dust in the wind,
I am out of sight.

I hollow the grave of shame,
I am the forgotten study,
I am the honest truth,
I am truly lonely.

I succumb to the wounds,
I am the ungodly,
I am the before and after,
I strive to be somebody.

I am who I am,
and soon I shall be earth,
still resting and ruminating,
while I wilt to dirt.

Ignorance is bliss
Only when knowing would hurt.

Who are you when no one's watching?

*Do you still apologise for being yourself?*

Subtle are the self-inflicted atrocities
I commit in the name of love.

# *Accepting*

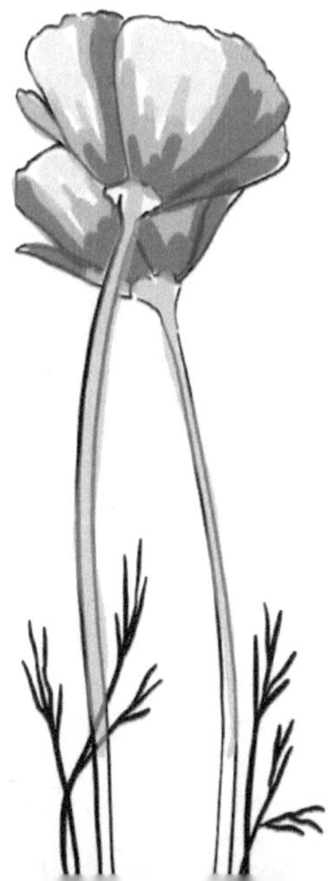

# *Normal*

I walk into the room confident, beaming and tall
In the split second that I see you
You look over at me, smile and I fumble
I try to be normal.

My normal consists of a skipped heartbeat,
My normal is a sensation of the butterflies burning up
with the speed of their wings flapping hard in my chest.

My normal consists of bursting clouds of confetti
When you laugh at something I said,
My normal is piercing needles in my spine
Trying to get me to stand up straight when I know I'm falling
for you.

My normal isn't the norm.
My normal isn't anything anyone should know about.

You look at me through the lenses of the telescope
it took your entire adolescence to create.
You look at me with the eyes of an unknown spectator.

While you speak through expressions,
your eyes and passionate depictions
I sit drawing out scenarios of how to
revive myself every time you take my breath away.

You ask me out of curiosity, I ask you,
Knowing the answers but only wanting to hear it
in your voice.
Every word you so creatively express and every feeling you emote, I passively relate to and resonate with.

My normal allows me to wear my smile like a safety vest as I dive into the ocean of your thoughts,
I swim into the depth of your conversations and believe I'm not drowning
But I did.

My normal is the shallowest of graves keeping my emotions buried for you
My normal is unrequited love and the slowest death I will ever face

For every time I walk into the room confident,
beaming and tall
In the split second that I see you
You look over at me, smile and I fumble
I try to tell you that I love you
But instead, I try to be normal.

## *Cliché*

The lower I took my standards for you
the lesser you made an effort for me,
and when I stepped back and asked for more
you took off and labelled me 'crazy'.

*you are the cliché I've read about.*

## *Examples*

I choose to live by the truth I've come by,
I've held onto my past too long,
I put my value and worth in the wrong hands
And waited for the right one to come around.

I've been thirsty, hungry and hanging by a thread,
I've waited for someone to save me,
My heart and legs shackled, hazy in the head
But no one wanted to believe me.

Throughout my life I've had choices of who not to be,
Imagine learning that as a kid,
No role models to unlock my potential with their key,
So faking it, is what I did.

I always said fake it till you make it,
Till I saw how far I walked in my torn down shoes,
No idols or examples to live by,
Not even a romanticised muse.

Every ounce of effort I put into my skill
Was met with critical thinking,
I tried to impress them by building castles in the sky
While my rusted boat stayed sinking.

So as I reach this stage of my blooming life,
I am a student and skilled apprentice,
I have crawled victorious out of life's lessons
With broken bones and bruised fists.

Don't worry my love if you're at a time
Where all hope seems gone and empty,
I lived through my own examples and-
I still have my whole life left in me.

Nothing brought me down harder to earth
than realising that people aren't the words they say,

*they are their actions.*

## To Be Heard

There are days where I talk a lot for someone who isn't heard,
And days where I overthink every single word,
There are days upon days where I don't say a thing,
Or add on to emotions that people tend to bring.

There have been moments of fleeting joy that I wave goodbye to everyday,
And moments of overwhelming sadness in
which I choose to stay,
There are ways to cope and move on, some
people calmly say,
Advice on how to skip past grief, I wish I could
obey.

The hardest pill of all that I am still to swallow,
Is that I feel so much, all while I thought I was hollow,
I felt my shoulders weighing me down with burdens that weren't mine,
And every time I fell apart, I stood back up saying 'I'm fine'.

The mirror of reality was held up to my face with confrontations that I feared,
And no matter how hard I fought it,
My buried emotions had reappeared.

I cried on some days and barely slept on the rest
I opened myself up to those who really weren't the best

I spoke about my feelings to close ones through therapy
I uttered words and spoke truths that didn't come easy to me.

It took every ounce and every piece of me to hold on
I shed all of me, all the years of shame I had worn
There are still days upon days where I don't say a thing,
Or add on to emotions that people tend to bring,

There are days when I think speaking about my life is absurd
But only once you've tried it, you know the power of being heard.

If you gave yourself as many chances as you give others,
You'd be disappointed a lot *lesser.*

## *101 Ways to Die*

I woke up one morning in an empty space,
Barren and void, not a thing, not a face,
I tried to remember when I got here and how,
Am I dead or still alive for now?

What did I do to get here today,
Retracing my steps might help in a way,
Was I in a building that collapsed?
Did I overdose after I relapsed?

Did I choke on something or did I laugh to death?
Did I slip in the bathroom or smoke too much meth?
I don't know how to swim so maybe I drowned?
Maybe I died of loneliness cause there's no one around?

Did I starve and die hungry or did I jump off a cliff?
Was I caught in an avalanche and then I froze stiff?
Maybe I was stabbed to death after I got raped,
Maybe I was buried alive and couldn't escape.

I would probably remember a burning house,
Maybe at the hands of a cheating spouse?
Did I take a bullet to the head?
Or did I break my neck falling off the bed?

Did I fall down the stairs or get run over by a truck?
Maybe a scorpion bit me and I ran out of luck?
Did I just kick it and not get up?
Were my spirit angels finally fed up?

Nothing comes to mind when I think of how I reached this place
Not a reason, no anger, no single thought to face,
But there's something in this air that I could breathe and borrow
I am free of burdens and all my human sorrow.

## *You're Next*

The skeletons of my past cling to my back,
As the insecurities of my present lay down the carpets,
Self-hate and Anxiety crush the walls to witness the scene,
My closet of wilted shame is tearing down its hinges;

*You're next,* says the therapist.

# Woman

Woman to woman
I come from a woman
I become a woman
And I birth a woman

Three generations of love, trauma, and blood
passed down,

*That only a woman would know how to heal from.*

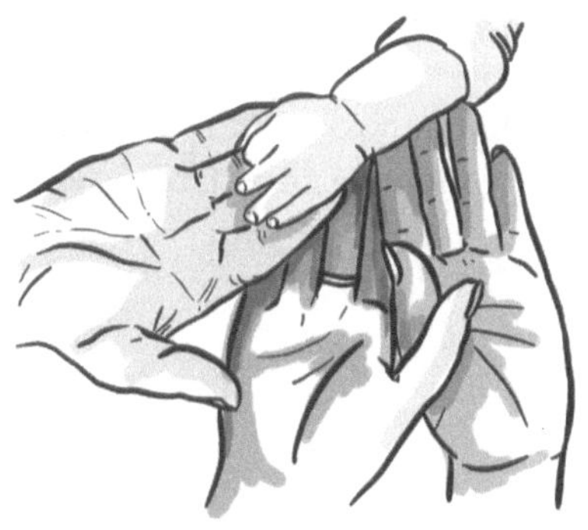

## *Someone Like You*

I have wanted to feel wanted in every clingy way,
I have wanted you to hold me close while pleading me to stay,
I have wanted you to protect me be it night or day,
I have wanted you to be honest but you aren't the words you say.

Trials and time have shown me your truth and your petty lies,
I thought you meant it when you wanted me to be your wife,
Slow was your exit and that jarring goodbye,
The one who promised to protect me was the one to make me cry.

So must I love myself from now and forget all I knew?
People say don't fall in love and I guess it may be true,
I should be moving on now, it's long overdue,
I hope to love again but never someone like you.

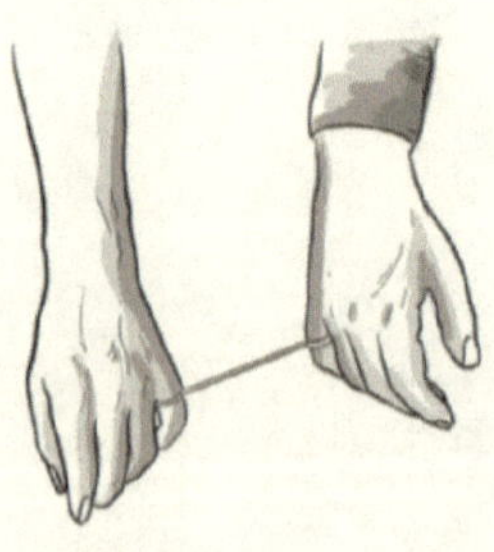

The day I get to my deathbed,
I will be closest to those I call my life.

## BPD

One day I feel too much,
The other, I feel nothing at all.
I could wait all day for you
And spend my last breath waiting for your call.

I could be the dream you dream,
But I am the nightmare I fear.
I feel like I'm living day to day
But I'm not really here.

I wash up on the shores of the memories I dread,
I run back and drown into the ocean of sleep,
I think all my problems would leave if I was dead,
And I wouldn't constantly open the wounds I keep.

I am the silence in the day,
I am the chaos in the night,
I am the disappearing act,
And I'm the lone silhouette in the light.

I could go 0 to 100 before you breathe,
I can forget myself and the people I need,
I have walked into fire and walked out broken,
I have swallowed the words I ought to have spoken.

I suffer from something so awful, my love,
You wouldn't want to come close to see,
I could give you my heart, my head and still,
You wouldn't understand a thing about me.

How little of you to think that I was too much.

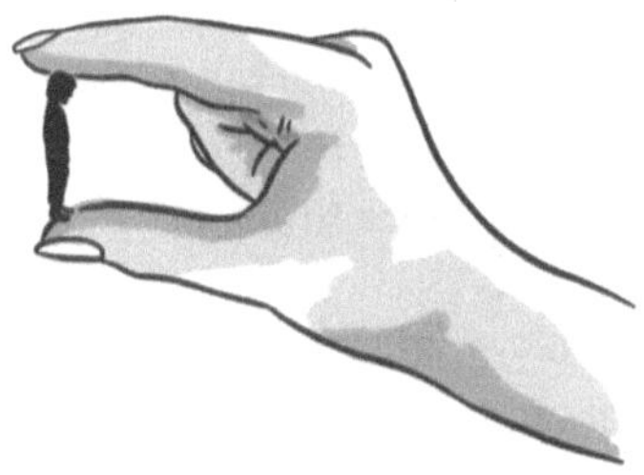

## *I Cry, I Cry*

I cry, I cry, I heave and I sigh,
Because I'm done with work,
I cry, I cry, I heave and I sigh,
Because work doesn't feel like work.

It feels like birth,
It feels like relief,
It fills me with grief
I cry, I cry, I heave and I sigh,

Because it shouldn't hurt.

I wake up to pain and ache,
I wake up to stay awake,
I cry, I cry, I heave and I sigh,
Because I need a break.

I need to be alone,
Somewhere off my phone,
Somewhere I can be,
anything but me,
I cry, I cry, I heave and I sigh.

Because it hurts to be.

Knowing, hurts more than all,
Thinking, feels like I'm about to fall,
I cry, I cry, I heave and I sigh,
Because this may be my call.

I'm drifting away,
Far from today,
From all that I've known,
And where I belong,
I cry, I cry, I heave and I sigh.

Because there's *no one home.*

## *Vase*

You were the vase in my life,
pretty, strong and empty,
with the potential to be so much more
but you have cracks in you.

*You could never hold the water long enough*
*to let my flowers bloom.*

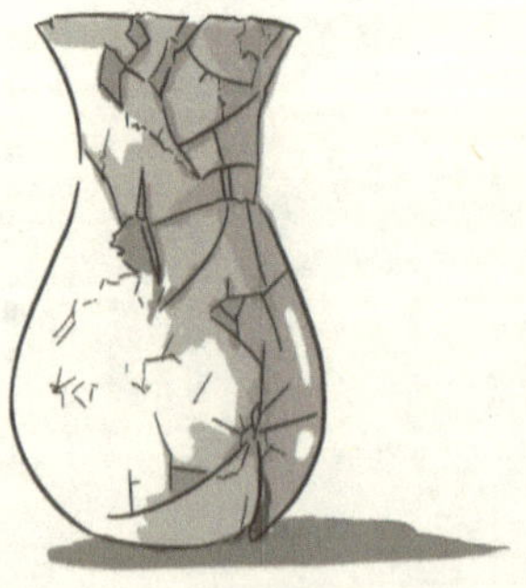

The flowers danced in the sunrays,
the moon seemed more white than grey,
the sky, the sea and all of me,
Felt a bit lighter today.

I saw the breeze in motion,
I felt the spray of the ocean,
The birds, the bees and all the tall trees,
Erupted with pure devotion.

I gazed at the cars driving by,
I hung all my clothes out to dry,
My wallet, my shoes and things I tend to lose,
Didn't choose to make me cry.

I met up with some close friends,
We reconnected and made amends,
My past, my present and every life lesson,
Shall guide me to the end.

So here's my loving call,
To the ones rising and the ones that fall,
For love, for hate, for too little too late,
You will survive it all.

So elevate to become who you admire,
Chase and achieve all that you desire,
Your strength, your love and all the above,
Will bend the universe into what you require.

## *Women*

If all the women before you
Were to see you cry,
Over an ordinary guy,
They'd hug you close and say,

'We planted our own trees before you were born and now,
You can pick out the flowers he never got for you.'

Ties are cut easier than tension

# *Afraid to Fall*

There's hope in silent moments.
There's peace in not knowing,
There's moving on and revenge.
There's maturity in growing,

There's failure in doubt,
There's opportunity in fear,
There's wisdom around the corner,
There's truth that's crystal clear,

There's tons to see in life,
And maybe none for free at all.
But there's no way you can fly,
If you're too afraid to fall.

## *Parts of Me*

There's parts of me written down,
Parts I still must write,
Parts in partial thoughts,
And parts in flight or fight.

There's seasons to my being,
Autumn, spring and snow,
Every leaf I shed for growth,
Is for lessons I've got to know.

I was once a bright student,
I was once dark in love,
I was a broken liar,
And afraid to change the above.

I have fought my battles alone,
I have held onto some friends,
I have been down in debt,
Unable to meet my ends.

I was a sore loser,
Too prideful and tough,
Till I lost it all,
And one win was enough.

Life has ways to humble you,
To teach you wrong from right,
I keep honesty beside me,
And hope as a beacon of light.

I have gained from my grief,
And earned from my loss,
I have let go of what left,
Never begged, never forced.

There's a truth in trials,
Why rock bottom helps you think,
Swim to the surface as a new you,
While the old you shall sink.

You shall emerge empty,
Free from all you know,
And what's better than starting over,
You can watch yourself grow.

## *Mother*

She is the morning sun
And the starry night,
She inspires happiness and joy,
She despises the spotlight.

Her charismatic aura
And her willingness to care,
Makes her the selfless one
Who tries to be everywhere.

She is the first one up,
The one to tuck everyone in,
Her silence muffles all her wants
And her needs within.

How I wish I could give to her,
Even half of what she did to me,
The sky, the stars, the world in her palm,
Just about the whole galaxy.

She was a child too once,
Someone with hopes and dreams like me,
She now lives them through us,
Oh what is this sacred sanctity?

She is undyingly loyal,
The happiest to serve,
The one who always looks for everything
Except the peace she deserves.

She is mother,
The only strength I see,
All of her metamorphoses'
Have resulted in all of me.

Now I must take the stand,
Follow in her reign,
So she can rest and enjoy the rest
And her efforts aren't in vain.

# *Adapting*

Slow is the journey to healing
for the skin they sewed onto you shall take years to shed.

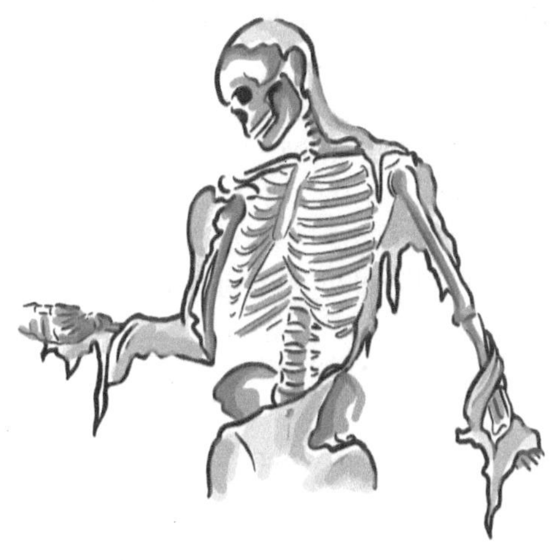

## *Listen*

Listen with a mind wide open
and a heart ungated,
with biases aside
and all breath bated.

listen to learn,
listen to know,
listen to cries for help,
listen to help them grow.

all you need to do is listen,

listen with the intent to understand,
listen with intrigue,
listen with concern and humility,
listen to just believe.

if you can lend your ears to one
and hear what they say,
you can read between the lines
and look through all they portray.

if all you do is listen,

you can hear an inner child crying,
a sigh of relief,
a small memory dying,
a spark of belief.

you can hear the whispers of joy,
the broken down dream,
the 30 year old who's still a boy
and the potential of all he could've been.

you can hear the fighting thoughts
and a heart that bleeds,
unexecuted plans
and their unmet needs.

in times like this where the loudest mouths have always spoken,
I have learnt to listen to the silent and broken,
for stories they tell are true to every word
and all of their stories deserve to be heard.

## *The Little Things*

I am a person looking for the little things,
I am just someone who waits,
not for the big gifts and grand gestures,
but for a big heart to enter my gates.

the heart who cares for me and loves to hear my laughter,
the heart that beats for me and not ten others on their roster.

the heart who'll remember birthdays,
and plan dates just for fun,
the heart that'll help out strangers,
and is kind in the long run.

the heart that understands that conflict
is a chance to grow,
the heart that doesn't run away
when it's feeling low.

The heart that communicates in volumes
and sheds all its skin,
the heart that accepts pure love and can go all in.

the heart that can be honest even when it all seems tough,
the heart that believes that it always truly is good enough,
the heart that melts my walls with the warmth it has to give,
the heart that believes in mistakes and is willing to forgive.

the heart that is okay with receiving more love than it can provide,
the heart that is so open with nothing in it to hide,
the heart that matches my pace with every step I take,
the heart that is brave enough to admit that it can make mistakes.

the heart that knows love is the fruit of your daily sowing,
the heart that can give a lot and hence keep growing,
the heart that knows the value of time well spent,
the heart that doesn't beat itself up and constantly repent.

the heart that can prioritize when things go to shit,
the heart that can walk away if we truly aren't a fit,
the heart that can put mine to rest and let me bloom into love,
the heart that makes it easy to do all of the above.

I'm looking for the little things,
that may not seem so little at times,
the heart I shall embed in me,
shall have to be deserving of mine.

## *I Remember*

There was a time when I saw things
For the first time.
Places I walked to, for the first time.
There are moments from my childhood that take me back
into those baby shoes crunching across the pebbled road.
The smell of moist mud and rain filled forests,
the sound of my mother's bangles and my father's footsteps.
I remember the smell of cigarettes on our water bottles at home.
I remember the box of smokes on the bathroom window sill.
I remember how I fit into the bucket like it was a bathtub.

I remember playing drums on the bowls on my kitchen floor
while being fed one airplane at a time.
The rush of adrenaline before a 100m race and
the burning heat in my body right after we ran.
The deafening sound of the gunshot and the loud cheering squad.
I have vague memories of being dropped to school and
running in before the first bell
I remember the chaos in the canteen by the candy stall
I can feel the texture of my textbooks my mother
used to cover with the brown paper before the year started.
I remember the weight of my bag like
The world rest on my shoulders.

I remember the sound of the last bell to send us home.
I remember the bus conductor handing me the small tickets every day.
I can feel the brakes of the bus slam hard
as I planted my feet firmly.
I remember the taste of the balloons while
I blew them up for birthday parties.
And the countless cakes I ate in celebration
I remember when making friends felt easy and
ignorance was bliss.
I remember my first kiss.
I remember how I was undressed the very first time
I remember how silent it was and how loud it felt to breathe
I remember dressing up by myself after.

I remember the scent of cologne water applied on a napkin
and held to my warm forehead when I had a fever
I remember my mother's warm hands rubbing vapour rub
into my chest and stomach when I had a cold.
I remember her feeding me all the way up into adulthood every time
I was sick.
I remember her telling me I would get better if I stayed off my phone.

I almost forget my good memories because I hold onto the wrong ones.
How could I forget the days I went horse riding as a child?
How could I ever forget my German shepherds and their litter of puppies?

How could I forget the day I smashed my forehead wide
open and got 8 stitches while I lay conscious.
I could never forget the taste of *kachhi kairi*, boar, jamun
and the countless salty spicy delights I ate as a child.

I remember being an individual.
I remember living my life. Free from thought and regret.
I want to remember more.
And I want to create memories today
That I can remember years from now.

*For the first time, I want to remember.*

## *I Think of You*

When the sunrays come through the window blinds,
When I find myself helpless and unkind,
When I have new memories and untold words on my mind,
I think of you.

I have thought of you on drives back home,
I have thought of you when I'm not alone,
I have thought of your number when I pick up my phone,
I have held you in my arms and etched that memory in stone.

I think of the moments, the words and the unspoken bond,
I think of you, where you are, deep into the night and beyond,

I smile at the images I was able to capture,
I think of you and unravel in rapture.

I think of you when I see how far I've come,
I think of you when I do everything you've done,

I've held onto the things you've held with your hands,
And stood in places where you used to stand.

I have thought of you when I couldn't think,
I've cried into nights and not slept a wink,
I have thought of holding you till night turned to day,
I think of you and how I wish you could stay.

Everyday life now seems like a test,
Before I wake and after I'm dressed,
Sitting at the table with all of our guests,
Looking at the empty chair where you used to rest,
*I think of you.*

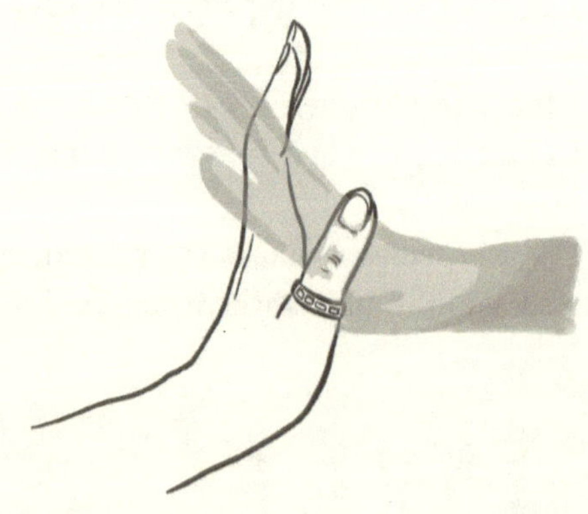

Patience might bring you gifts that perseverance overlooked.

## *Hold On*

I know now what they meant
When they said good things come to those who wait,
I keep checking my calendar to see
How close we are to our next date.

I replay the memories I have with you
Like a movie in my mind,
4k with crystal clear sound,
The theatre-quality kind.

Your face feels familiar on my fingertips
Cause I mapped you out so well,
Don't know when I'll see you next
But I remember how fragrant you smell.

Imagining the curves of your body
And the warmth of your skin takes me to another place,
A different time, a better moment.
When I can finally kiss your face.

Our time will come my love
And we will meet again somehow,
Hope and memories is all we have
So hold onto that for now.

The intimacy of taking my glasses off my face and
putting them on yourself
While asking 'Do I look good?'

Do you think droplets add to the beauty of roses?
Or were they not beyond beautiful to begin with?

## *Moments*

I've walked on lakes made of fire
And roads made of ice,
I've talked to children that are mean
And elders that are nice.

I've sat alone in the park
And felt lonely in crowded rooms,
I've plucked flowers in the dark
And stolen moments from the moon.

I've eaten and been sick
And starved to feel better,
I've ignored plenty calls
And blamed it on the weather.

I've met pets better than people
And learnt school isn't fun,
I've had cramps in my stomach
Right before meeting someone.

I've stepped on roses
And I've napped on grass,
I've dodged plenty bullets
And I've tasted broken glass.

I've had sleepless nights
And I've slept through the day,
I've had people tell me they're right
While they pushed me away.

I've had moments filled with tears
And those with joy that barely last,
I've come to face my fears
And I've come to terms with my past.

I've been through miles of happy forests
And dense meadows of pure sorrow,
I know no matter how bad today gets
I'll always look forward to tomorrow.

I have moved in every direction but ahead
I guess that's the con with having your walls up.

Let go of what no longer serves you,
allow distance between you and what betrays you,
speak the words that haunt you,
to the people that hurt you,
forgive those making efforts that move you,
forget those whose actions broke you,
acknowledge the qualities that make you,
introspect on patterns that shake you,
remember things they said to you,
bask in the fire they made for you,
dance in the floods designed to drown you,
do not fall for lies when they crown you,
laugh in the rooms they speak of you,
cry in the open, it's not weak of you,
lest you forget what was done to you,
lest you forget what they took from you,
every morsel of your bones that made you,
will fight the battles they bring to you,
your will and strength persist in you,
your beauty and pain rest in you,
if only they could see the real you,
the broken but truly brave you,
the love they would fill in you
would prove to be too much for you,
so all you need is more from you,
all your love and more to you.

# To Be an Artist

I am imploding into creations close to fatality,
When I feel the sadness take over me, I write,
I know not when to stop for I have to achieve immortality,
When I feel the chilling anxiety, I fight.

I feel the metaphorical fire burst out of me when I dance,
an inexplicable roar of steps,
when I am drowning in unpleasant memories by chance,
I sing as loud as it gets.

Some days when I feel the artistic itch,
I get out my needles and thread,
I put on my glasses & begin to stitch
Till everything goes silent in my head.

Unusual shall be the day when I have no desire,
No need or want to paint,
That's the day I cross the wire,
And meditate like a holy saint.

But on days I want the utmost peace,
I turn to the wheel as a potter,
The gliding hand, the spinning clay,
All bound together with water.

A few months down the line you see,
I resort to body ink,
A permanent piece of art on me,
Self-tattooed in a wink.

If I was not an artist,
I don't know who I'd be,
So many coping mechanisms,
That help make me, ME.

Every single thought I have,
Consequently relates to art,
There shall always be art in an artist,
Till death do us apart.

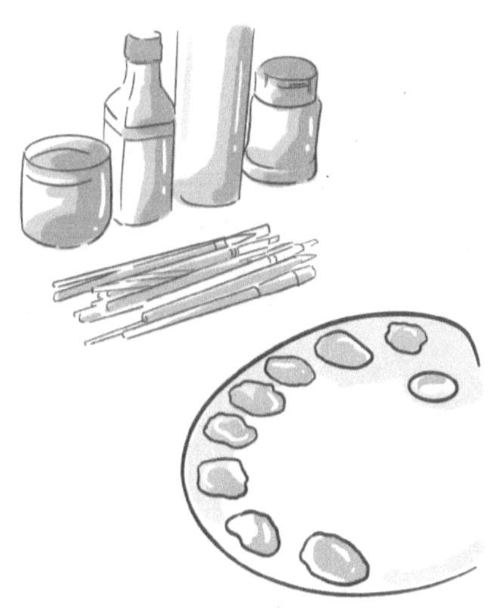

## *Sisters*

Some sisters share their outfits,
Some twin when they exercise,
Some sisters bully and borrow things,
Some don't leave your side.

Some sisters leave for college,
Some help you babysit your kids
Some sisters hold your hair up,
While you throw up on toilet lids.

Some sisters come years later,
In some shape, wave or form,
Some are not from your mother,
But feel like yours all along.

I was lucky to get a sister,
One random sunny day,
I've known her 8 years now,
And she always knows what to say.

She fills my heart with joy,
She is my safest place,
She loves me for who I am everyday,
And I light up when I see her face.

There is love in the world, I'm sure of it,
One that I won't have to beg for and find,
Because she shows me love every single day,
And that's truly one of a kind.

# *Meant for Me*

I walk on roads we used to,
And I sit on the sun kissed shoreline,
The warmth of the sun reminds me of you,
And how I called you mine.

Time moved on and we fell apart,
Hoped we would still find our way back.
I wish I could run back to the start,
Since there's so much left to unpack

I take a moment to reflect,
At things I've lost along with time,
If it's meant to be and meant for me.
I, once again shall call you mine.

what breaks you won't heal you,
what loves you won't leave you.

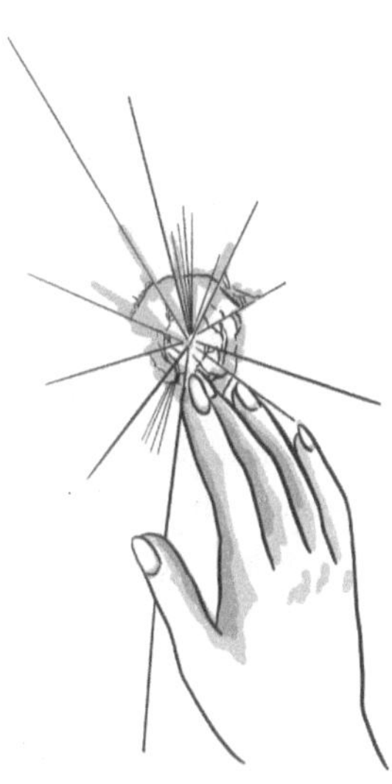

# *What I Want*

I want to fly over clouds
I want to swim across seas,
I want my parents to be proud
but I still want to be me.

I want to eat and not gain weight,
I want to run while I sit,
I want to rise early but sleep late,
I want to be lazy & stay fit.

I want to be the one who leaves
but I want to commit and be there,
I want modesty up my sleeve
with my riches stashed somewhere.

I want to love and not cry,
I want to be the centre of attention,
I want to ignore everyone
and still make a good connection.

I want to have a lot of things
and there's so much I wish to be,
but despite all the conflict,
I still want to be me.

## Physical Touch

You hold my waist in your sweet embrace,
You feel so warm and right,
All my defences defenceless against you,
I have no will to fight.

You caress my chest, my breast and moan,
There's all of me for you,
Your hands circle my belly and hips,
Oh how you make me cum for you.

You pull my hair and say things out loud,
I close my eyes and focus on task,
My brain riddled with butterflies,
While you thrust and make me gasp.

Your hands lower onto my cheeks,
Slide on my lips and ease right into me,
You ate me for breakfast lunch and dinner,
Even for evening tea.

So tenderly you whisper while you look into my eyes,
I can barely hold a thought and then you flip me in surprise.

I'm face down in a pillow,
Clutching on for dear life,
Are you a fucking cowboy?
Cause you're taking me on a ride.

In your final push,
I feel a rush so deep,
Your forehead close to mine,
And then we fall asleep.

You kiss me into the night and
Are gentle with aftercare,
The way you separate my soul from my body,
I forgot who I am and where.

And now you close your eyes,
The time is ten past eleven,
I run my fingers through your hair,
And Baby, you feel like heaven.

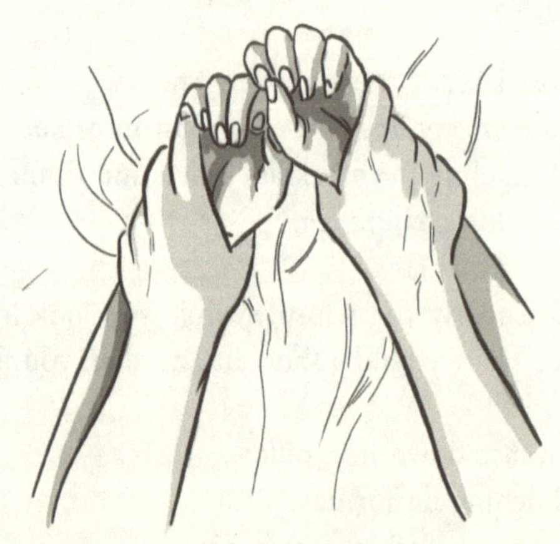

## Balloons

I remember the first time you blew up a balloon and handed it to me,
It was the lightest gift filled with the deepest pleasure you could ever give me.
The balloon didn't stay around for too long though;
I popped it close to my face so that I could feel your breath on my lips
*Once again.*

## *I Am Home*

I am home.
there was no chase,
no map, no road, no path,
nothing that led me to believe I would find love.

nothing that hinted at the magnitude of the storm
you would create within the walls of my heart,
there was no fence of protection I could keep up with you,
no walls strong enough to contain the force you became.

I would not have known the voice of reason,
the depth of understanding,
the strength in trust
or the effortless love with which I love you
every single day had I not met you.

I look forward to waking up
with the memory of a yesterday with you
and the hope of a blissful tomorrow.
I fall into the arms of your safe haven
with weak knees because I know to trust now.

I can be fragile, I can be feminine, I can be vulnerable,
for I know, you know love.
I have chosen to embrace my faults
and own up to them on my knees in front of you,

you have seen me bear with my shortcomings written on my sleeves,
I have torn the flesh of my past to grow into a new person that I can love first, before you do.

I had been lost for so long,
no map, no road, no path,
that would lead me to believe
that I could find a safe place to be
but now I am home.

*You are home.*

The other day I saw myself in someone else,
and couldn't decide if I should offer my help
or compliment her strength.

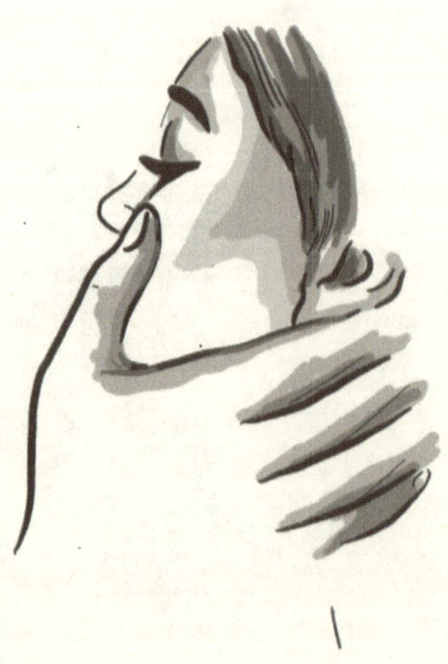

# *Friendships*

My friendships have meant so much to me,
Lifetime subscriptions and mostly stress free,
More than two and less than eight,
There's so much, in them, to appreciate.

They know how I talk, walk and move,
My impulsiveness and foreboding attitude,
They comfort my monsters and keep my nightmares at bay,
And let my inner child come out to play.

My friends know how to comfort me in grief,
Although our texting and calls may be brief,
They know how to navigate through the tough bits,
They keep their heads and use their wits.

When life tends to get more than they can manage,
They open up and empty out all of their baggage,
I have seen them for their flaws, imperfections and sins,
And also their growth, their kindness and wins.

Friendships to me mean giving more than I can borrow,
And knowing I'll be supported tenfold tomorrow,
And if everything in my life goes out of control and away,
Rest assured my friends are always here to stay.

## *Finger on the Trigger*

And there were days where I waited
for you to ask if I'd take a bullet for you
because I'd say yes.

*Dying for you is far less painful than watching you*
*with your finger on the trigger while you say love me.*

## Strangers

These days I seek out strangers and people I barely know,
Unbiased, unaware and clueless ones with who I can grow.

I speak my mind and share my stories
Not fearful of familiar disapproval.
I find comfort in the unknown
But maintain boundaries that are crucial.

There is something about a new viewpoint
That whips your brain about,
their new ideas and new principles.
Nothing to create irrational self-doubt.

Like a breath of fresh air
They enter your life and stay,
They make you regret your comfort zone
And teach you how to play.

Strangers come into your life
To show you things you missed.
I have trusted a stranger with my secrets
But have a friend who'd never see that list.

That which leaves always makes way for what's better

Upon the hill she sat and watched the green grass sway.
She journeyed on for hours and hours to get to where she was today.
She was told not to travel alone, 'You don't know what it's like out there'
'You don't know how the world works, you're too dumb and unaware'

She tightened the straps of her backpacks
And off and on she went
She sat alone, off her phone and thought about the time she'd spent
With people who weren't here to see
How good she felt to at last be free

She spoke to strangers here and didn't overthink
She smiled and pushed her comfort zone to the very brink
Her tightly wound noose was finally cut loose,
And so she could breathe like before
The sticks and stones that broke her bones
Couldn't hurt her anymore

She thought back on how it felt to be silenced
And alone in a crowded space,
Her enthusiasm and her joy,
Was wiped right off of her face

She was told to be quiet when they decided on how their stay should be,
Broken up right after, there goes her laughter, but it is what it's got to be.

So how does she move on with life and smile through their fall?
She knows her worth isn't measured by their words
and she was the lucky one after all.
Her steps had a purpose in them now that she walked by herself once more
She made it to the top and life came to a stop
When this memory went to her core.

Her tears shed and out she cried, she had never felt this safe,
And it was on that hill, she discovered, she is her own safe space.

So despite what they've told you,
Maybe tried to scold you,
Saying traveling alone isn't a choice
Do not succumb to the glares and go numb,
You still have your own voice.

I hope you get to see,
Everything you can be,
If you just let yourself go
Life is so much more when you walk out the door,
From the person who always says 'no'.

You took half my life to make me who I am today
And now I must take the other half to undo it all.

## *I's In Love*

Indulge in love
The platonic love, the self-love,
The I-love-how-this-feels love.

Invest in love
The long term love, the childhood love,
The I-could-give-you-everything love.

Investigate in love
The curious love, the mysterious love,
The Is-this-okay-with-you love?

Impress in love
The gracious love, the respectful love,
The I-remembered-you-like-this love.

Inspire in love
The generous love, the competitive love,
The we-have-each-other's-backs love.

Include in love
The considerate love, the kind love,
The I-want-you-to-be-there love

Initiate in love
The gentle love, the budding love,
The I-want-to-get-to-know-you love.

To be in love and stay in love
Practice all your I's in Love

## *The Mother in Me*

Everyday I'm so afraid of how I'll live tomorrow.
How I'll survive, who will be around me and where my steps will take me.
I sit perched on my window thinking of the countless possibilities of how I could live out my nightmare of being inadequate as a parent.

How I may not be enough when more is asked of me. If I were to find the love of my life who treats me well and makes me question my own sanity, If I were to birth the most normal beautiful child, would I be enough?

Would I be a passionate mother and a loving wife? Will I have to abandon my profession that has made who I am today? Where will I turn if I turnout like those I was afraid of? What if I self-fulfil my prophecies of being mediocre and inept?

This builds in me like boiling lava, simmering till I erupt into descending manic thoughts spiralling out of control while I console myself
'but you won't'
'You will be so much better.'

I proceed into a monologue in my mind while I crouch with my head between my arms

You have so much love to give, you have learnt to provide, to nurture,
To forgive, to care and to remain still, you have learnt to stay.
A child needs their parent to stay.

A child needs presence, praise, persistence, providers and protection.
A child needs everything that you know you are capable of being.
You have a mother in you.
You have always been a nurturer,

You parented your parents, your sibling, your pets and your plants.
You tried to be what you wished you had as a child.
You set yourself to the highest standard of forgiveness and the highest pedestal of perfection so you could be who you could have relied on.

You move mountains in love. You believe in love.
You know that a child's first footsteps to you and their last goodbyes to you will outlive your own memories in your mind.
Life moulded you into the person you needed so you know what a parent means to a child.

You know the consequences of good examples and of bad ones.
You know a child grieves the death of a parent if the idea of safety is lost to them.
Because you did.

But now, you move through life, loving and leading by example.
Knowing the worth of relationships, the value of bonds made in blood
And the duty that comes with it.
A mother was made out of you the day you learnt
That a child will search for love everywhere, even into adulthood,
If love isn't shown to them when they are young.

You know how to love.
You know what it takes to love someone more than oneself.
You are the ingredients in the perfect quantities that it takes to make a mother.

*All you need is to believe.*

# About the Author

SANAYA IRANI is a multidisciplinary artist and a poet based in Mumbai. She started writing poems when she was in school and hasn't stopped since. Poetry and painting have been her lifelong methods of self-expression and she finds them to be helpful creative outlets for any pent-up feelings.

Irani is a professional artist and business owner, having worked with a series of brands on multiple projects in the categories of mural designing, illustrations, canvas paintings, make-up and hair artistry, tattoo artistry and digital conceptualizing. She has also designed for clothing brands and customized sneakers as well.

As a poet, she has always used her own life experiences to create lyrical and narrative poems, which tend to resonate with individuals with similar life experiences. Recently, after getting diagnosed with ADHD, autism, depression and BPD, a lot of Irani's life and the reasons for why she was a certain way became clear to her. Therapy and her inner support system have always been her biggest motivator to boost her morale and keep her going.

In her free time, Irani enjoys travelling, writing, painting, trying out new food, playing video games, watching true crime documentaries, weightlifting, bike riding, getting tattoos done, playing racket sports and, occasionally, hiking.

This is her first book of poems and illustrations.

www.ingramcontent.com/pod-product-compliance
Lightning Source LLC
La Vergne TN
LVHW090518110826
845146LV00003B/907

*9789355437822*